GOAL
SETTING

The 8-step process to greatness

Table of Contents

INTRODUCTION

The premise of this book is to provide a palatable framework for young people aged 13-18 years old to aid in their development of goal setting. This book, along with the other books within our series, will help our readers on their journey to becoming self-sufficient. It is highly encouraged, if available, that a parent, guardian and/or mentor read this book alongside the reader. We are making this request as it will help spur conversation as well as help add extra context to the content within each chapter.

CHAPTER 1

~ ~ ~

Establishing Mindset

Before we begin, we should first define what a mindset is. We define mindset as the way in which you process and respond to the world around you. The reason why this is listed as the first step to goal setting is due to the fact that all things start in the mind. Think of your mind as a seed. If you have a good/ healthy seed, the likelihood of you having a fruitful harvest is increased. If you have a bad seed, the likelihood of you not having a harvest to begin with is also increased. In short, if you think and move in positivity, the chances are higher that you will receive positivity in return.

While establishing a mindset is an easy task to do, the hard part is to determine what you will steer that mindset towards. Take note that everyone is unique which means that your mindset will also be unique. Therefore, do not worry if you and your friend have your eye on accomplishing the same goal but that your route to achieving that goal is different. The most important factor in this is that you establish a mindset on positivity and ensure that you are being true to yourself.

Scenario: *You are in a relationship. This person feels like they are the love of your life. The person breaks up with you because they are interested in dating someone else.*

Example (negative mindset): You take the breakup really hard and you are crushed. You feel that there is no one else in the world that can compare and you vow to never date again.

Example (positive mindset): You take the breakup really hard and you are crushed. You feel that there is nothing else in the world. So you decide to take some time to work on yourself. You take all of your negative and sad emotions and you focus it on positivity and internal growth.

As you can see from the scenario above, we all encounter negative experiences in life. Whether it is a failing grade on a test or termination from a job, negative experiences can cause feelings of self-doubt, failure and depression. All of which can cause you to feel like giving up. Developing a mindset of positivity on the other hand, will allow you to find the light in these situations. In times when you have a poor outcome, try to find the lesson so that you can learn and grow from the situation. Learning from negativity can go a long way in your journey of developing a stronger positive outlook on life. Taking time to self-reflect and grow from your experiences are some of the tools that will empower your future success. The mindset we encourage you to have is simple: Think positive, seek growth and good things will follow.

CHAPTER 2

⌒⌒⌒

Developing Resolve

Resolve is defined as your ability to keep going despite the situation or circumstances. The reason why resolve is so important to have is because many things can occur in life that will derail you. Simply put "Life happens". The sooner you realize that life cannot be controlled and bent to your will, the easier it will be to accept things as they come. With that said, it does not mean that you should allow things to happen to you.

After you cultivate your mindset, be sure to understand that there will be things on your journey that will distract you. Knowing that this is a constant part of life is crucial as you can start to mentally prepare for the unknown. Notice how I said "prepare" and not avoid it. This is a major key to being successful as preparation will enable you to continue moving forward even when things are looking bleak or, at the very least, allow you to continue moving forward even if you do get sidetracked.

Scenario: You set a goal of making the basketball team and in order to make it, you know that you will need to practice shooting drills daily for one hour. You have 1 month to prepare for tryouts.

Example (lack of resolution): The first week of your plan goes smoothly. The second week you find that there is a party on the weekend and your friends want to hang out during your practice time. You have spent an entire week practicing and miss hanging out with your friends, so you decide to skip your shooting drills for the week. Since you skipped your shooting drills for the 2nd week you notice that during your third week of practice you are sluggish and not performing as well during your drills. Based on your bad third week of practice, you give up altogether on your fourth week and decide to skip trying out for the team all together since you realized that you would not make the cut due to you not being prepared.

Example (having resolved): The first week of your plan goes smoothly. The second week you find that there is a party on the weekend and your friends want to hang out during your practice time. You have spent an entire week practicing and miss hanging out with your friends so you decide to hang out with your friends after your shooting drills as well as decide to start your shooting drills earlier in the day so you could attend the party. During the third week of shooting drills you continued to improve and realized that the time of your shooting drills didn't matter as long as you prioritized the practice each and every day. Your fourth week went off without a hitch as you did not skip any days of practice and when it came time for tryouts you scored the most points and obtained 2 triple doubles. A week later the coach posted the sheet of the players who made the team and you realized that you made the team.

As you can see in the example above, having resolve allowed for the goal to be accomplished. That scenario exemplified that no matter what life throws at you as a distraction, as long as you prioritize your goal and work through the obstacles that you can still achieve it. Oftentimes it can feel as though there is no end in sight when you run into a rough patch. Developing resolve and perseverance through difficult situations requires that you keep your end goal in mind. It is important to not just allow negative events to happen to you but to do something about it. Having resolve will help you power through these moments. Not only in trying times is it important to practice resolve but in the good times too. It is easy to let your foot off the gas and coast when you are in a good place. It is important to continue doing the work as well as enjoy your life along the way. Cultivating your mindset to remain positive enables for positive things to occur but this can be reinforced if you cultivate the resolve to stay the course.

CHAPTER 3

❧

Formulate the Plan

As the saying goes, "Fail to plan, plan to fail". Planning can differ from person to person. Before you take the time to create a plan you must first identify what it is that you would like to accomplish. If you don't know what you want then it will be impossible to obtain it. Now that your end goal has been identified you can start the process of figuring out what steps you will take to achieve your personalized goal. One of the most important pieces of putting a plan together is to understand yourself and create a process that is realistic and blends with your personality. The reason why we call this out is that creating an unrealistic plan is the easiest way to never reach your goal.

Goal setting

Identifying what your goal is can be difficult if you have never done it before. If this is your first time creating a goal, simply ask yourself, "What do I want?". Figuring out what you want allows for the vision to start taking shape. From there, ask yourself, "Why do I want this?". Knowing your "why" will enable you to continue pushing through despite any setbacks. The last question would be, "When do I want it?". This question takes things a bit further as you are now able to set a date for accomplishing the goal. Once those three questions are asked then you can start the process of narrowing down any specifics that make this goal special to you.

The more specific the goal the easier it is to achieve. After you have visualized the end result that you want, the next step would be to write it down. This is where knowing, "When you want it" comes in because then you can start working backwards from your goal and date. Regardless of how big or small your goals are, be sure to write them out no matter what. Remember that your goals are personal to you and do not have to reflect the goals of other people.

After the what, why and when of your plan have been identified, the next step is to start formulating the plan. For example, if your goal is to create a fashion line of sneakers by August 1st, you may achieve this goal by sketching designs daily, going to look at fabrics three days a week and sewing every other day. No matter what tasks you set, make sure that they align with the end goal and that you are accomplishing something at least every week so that momentum is maintained. A good way to organize your objectives is to create a short or long-term strategy. This allows for the planning to remain nimble but continue to move forward.

Short term planning

For all intents and purposes, we will define short term planning as any time that is 3 months or less. As you continue to learn and master this concept, feel free to extend this time out, but in general, short term planning is typically looked at as 1 year or less. Due to the time being so condensed for short-term planning you must make sure that your goals are structured in a way that you can accomplish things in a timely manner. With time being of the essence be prepared to act immediately on your plan. We recommend setting an objective for yourself daily regardless of how small it may seem. It is easy to give up on your plan, especially if you have not invested much time and energy into it so make sure to set your objectives, work on them daily, and most importantly remember to keep pushing through despite any distractions or daily fluctuations in feelings.

Long term planning

Long term planning is generally defined as any time frame longer than a year but for this book, let's define long term planning as any time longer than 3 months. As you continue to master this concept, start to challenge yourself by expanding this timeframe out. The advantage of long-term planning is that you have time on your side. This is because you have more time to achieve your goal which means that your objectives can also be spaced out further if you choose to do so. Just make sure that you understand that this can also be a disadvantage if you do not leverage your time wisely. Therefore, you must be disciplined in following the objectives that you have set for yourself. Just as we recommend setting daily goals for short term planning, we are recommending that you set weekly goals for long term planning. While it would still be ideal to work on tasks daily, we understand that this could also cause feelings of exhaustion which may turn into you abandoning your goal altogether. Remember, the most important thing to do when creating a plan is to follow through and to continue working at your set pace.

Define your benchmarks (criteria for success)

The objectives you established during your planning are crucial to success. Objectives will act as a check and balance system for you to make sure you stay the course and hold yourself accountable. Outside of having your plan and objectives identified, you should establish a criteria for success. This is important because it will allow you to measure how well you are aligning to accomplish your goal. For example, you may set a goal and establish targets but as you continue to work you may realize that even if you are following your plan as you laid it out that your results may not be what you thought they would be. Therefore, adding benchmarks to your targets will enable you to see how well you are truly doing with accomplishing your goals.

Scenario: *You have an important event coming up in 6 weeks and you would like to lose 6 lbs so your outfit will fit better. You figured that if you set a caloric intake goal and work out five days a week, this will help to achieve that goal.*

Example (poor planning): In order to meet your goal you have decided to meet your target by losing one pound a week. Two weeks pass and you realize that you gained 3 lbs. You continue working out but you are still unsure as to why you are gaining weight but you decide to continue pursuing this goal. Another three weeks have passed and you have only lost one pound. You feel so discouraged that you spent five weeks trying to lose weight only to gain weight. You give up on your goal and decide to skip your event.

Example (planning well): In order to lose 6 lbs., you have decided to do so by losing one pound a week. You set a specific goal of eating fewer calories a day than you are burning by tracking all of the food you're eating as well as implanting a structured 6week cardio program. After two weeks you lose 3 lbs and so you decide to stay on task and continue with your outlined eating and workout plan. After 6 weeks you end up losing 8 lbs and look fantastic at the event.

As you can see in the example above, it is very important to establish metrics along with your goals. If it wasn't for setting the weekly targets and goals, the person in the example would not have known if the plan was working and if they needed to make adjustments. Planning for success is not always easy and will require a positive mindset and resolve. It is important to learn how to set goals that are specific and truly reflect who you are and where you are trying to go. Keep your plan simple and practical with very clear benchmarks along the way.

CHAPTER 4

~~~

Take Action

This step is the simplest to comprehend at face value but is also one of the hardest to enact. Most people find it easy to talk about what they want or will do but seldom do they do it. The reason why "taking action" is the easiest step to comprehend is because you are simply doing just that…taking action. What makes this step hard for many people is that they often skip the step before this one which is to create a plan. We started chapter 3 off with "fail to plan, plan to fail" for a reason. In order to take action, you must first know what it is that you want to do then you must actually do it!

Scenario: *You want to buy your first car within the next 6months and it will cost you $3000.*

Example (lack of action): You make a short term plan to get a job at the local grocery store and work 20 hours a week and save half of every paycheck. Your long-term goal is to increase your savings to 70% after three months. You begin working your job and the shifts are long. You see your friends less and less because they hang out during your working hours. Eventually you cut your hours from 20 down to 10 because work was getting in the way of hanging out. After three months, you have only $500 saved. You begin to feel like you are working for nothing and you eventually quit and catch a ride with your friends instead of getting your own car.

Example (taking action): You make a short-term plan to get a job at the local grocery store and work 20 hours a week and save half of every paycheck. Your long-term goal is to increase your savings to 70% after three months. You begin working your job and the shifts are long. You see friends less and less because they hang out during your working hours. You continue to work 20 hours a week and after three months you have hit your benchmark of saving half of the money. You continue to increase your savings as planned. After 6 months you will have the money to purchase the car.

As you can see in the example above, it is equally important to create a plan as it is to take action. Taking action does not count if you start something and do not finish it. Taking action means seeing the task all the way to completion. There may be times when you fall off schedule and/or miss a benchmark but do not get discouraged; the following chapters will discuss how to make necessary changes to plans. If you take the time to create a plan, you owe it to yourself to try and see it through as you will benefit the most from accomplishing your goals.

CHAPTER 5

~⁓~⁓~

Measure Results

While it is important to have the resolve to relentlessly push through, there is such a thing as being on a road to nowhere. When you create your plan and define your benchmarks the goal is to define your journey and what it looks like when you get there. Taking action is extremely important for the road to success but if you do not measure your results you will never know if the action you are taking is truly working. The step of measuring results goes hand in hand with defining your benchmarks. Think of these two steps as being different sides of the same coin.

Scenario: *You have a test coming up in 2 weeks and you are worried that you won't pass.*

Example (doesn't measure results): Since you have a test coming up, you decide to study for 30 minutes a day for the first week and then increase your study time to 1 hour for the week of the test. You are feeling confident since you have spent so much time studying and when you take the test you realize that you studied the wrong things. After the test was submitted you received a failing grade.

Example (measures results): Since you have a test coming up, you decide to study for 30 minutes a day for the first week. After 3 days of studying, you decide to measure your results by taking a quiz and you found out you were not studying the correct material. Based on your discovery, you decide to increase your study time to one hour as well as study the appropriate content for the test. A few days before the test you decide to take another quiz to measure how well you know the material and realize that you are more than ready for the test and therefore decide to decrease your study time back down to 30 minutes since you knew the material. The day of the test you are feeling confident and when you saw the questions you breezed through it. After submitting the test, you received your results and found out that you passed the test and received one of the highest grades in the class.

As stated in chapter 3, the purpose of defining benchmarks is to understand what your checkpoints are to ensure that you are tracking appropriately towards your goal. Measuring results comes into play by ensuring that the action you have been taking is hitting your benchmark targets. By measuring results, you will be able to know if you should stay the course or if you need to take a different course of action. No matter how confident you are in accomplishing your goal, be sure to NEVER skip this step as this step will be crucial in saving you time. If you realize that your current actions are not helping you achieve your goals, do not be afraid to go back to chapter 3 to adjust your plan.

CHAPTER 6

~⁓~

The Pivot – Don't Be Afraid to Try Something New

The pivot is one of the most important steps that one can take. It gives you the grace to know that it is ok to adjust how you tackle your plan. While it is great to have resolve in pushing through the hardships, it is important to pivot when need be. We created this book to help guide you along your journey of setting and accomplishing goals. The biggest lesson to learn about accomplishing goals is to focus on the end result more than the journey of how you get there.

Oftentimes when people create immensely detailed plans they become a slave to it. Being a slave to your plan means that you have mapped out every fine detail therefore you are fixated on the idea that you can only accomplish your goal if you follow it in the order in which you laid out. This could cause one to go on an emotional rollercoaster and eventually quit after a few hurdles due to the amount of unnecessary pressure that they placed on themselves. What we are teaching is to focus MORE on the end result and LESS on the exact path as this sets the tone in your mind to remain nimble in your approach. On your road to success, there will be plenty of hurdles and if you become too fixated on a set road then you are more likely to fail once that road becomes rough.

Measuring your results will help you to evaluate where you are in your journey of achieving your goal. Sometimes after you measure your success along the way, you may not get the results you wanted. You may realize you have fallen off the path of achieving your goal. At this point, it is important to analyze what has brought you to this conclusion and how you can change your approach to get back on course. Pivoting is just that, a chance to correct and get back on track after assessing where you currently are.

Scenario: *You have signed up for a 4-mile run that is 8 weeks away. You set a goal to finish the run in under 35 minutes.*

Example of poor pivot: You plan to run a mile per day and then increase your runs by a quarter of a mile every week. You also plan to measure your results on the third week with a target of running 2 miles in under 15 minutes. You follow your plan exactly and on the third week, you ran 2 miles in 22 minutes. You decide that you probably just had a bad day, and you continue your original plan of adding just a quarter mile every week to your daily runs. You intend to do this before the race. When race day comes, you finish the 4-mile run in 50 minutes and fail to meet your target.

Example of a good pivot: You make a plan to run a mile per day and then increase your runs by a quarter of a mile every week. You also plan to measure your results on the third week with a target of running 2 miles in under 15 minutes. You follow your plan exactly and on the third week, you ran 2 miles in 22 minutes. You decide to pivot and begin running at least 2.5miles a day and you add 1mile every week until the race. You plan to measure your results again in two weeks in hopes that you can run 3 miles in 25 min. Within two weeks you met your goal of running 3 miles in 25min. You will continue to train and follow your new plan. Race day is a success, and you finish the 4 mile run in 33 minutes.

As life changes, you must change. Pivot is a tool that enables access to other paths on your journey to accomplishing your goals. Staying fixated on the result and not the path allows you more creative freedom and ultimately more peace in knowing that when one door closes that another will open…in due time. The key is to never stop pursuing your goal(s) but to always be willing to adjust your plan when the time comes. The next chapter will help you with coping with any perceived failures that you face along the way.

CHAPTER 7

~~~

Embrace Failure

Learning to accept failure as a part of life will empower you beyond belief. This is because it enables you to learn from your failures. Learning from past mistakes allows you to know what to avoid as well as what to do differently going forward. It has been normalized that failure should be avoided at all costs, but this couldn't be further from the truth. Through failure, you can develop resolve and character.

Scenario: *You have your first piano recital in three weeks and must learn to play three songs.*

Example (didn't embrace failure): You begin practicing each song by yourself every other day for your recital. You measure your ability to play the songs by having your piano teacher listen in as you practice. The feedback from the teacher is that you did well but could tell that you were nervous while playing. The recital comes and again, you get nervous, which results in you messing up several times throughout your performance. You are disappointed that you could not take control of your nerves and instead of working on your anxiety which is caused by playing in front of people you decide to quit completely because you feel ashamed.

Example (embraced failure): You begin practicing each song by yourself every other day for your recital. You measure your ability to play the songs by having your piano teacher listen in as you practice. The feedback from the teacher is that you did well but could tell that you were nervous while playing. The recital comes and you get nervous, you mess up several times throughout your performance. You are disappointed. You decide that you will continue to play piano and work on your performance anxiety. Before your next recital, you decide to challenge yourself by playing piano in front of anyone who will listen to you. Confronting your failure head on pushed you to new heights and enabled you to calm any fears that you have during your next performance.

Failure is a constant in life. Just as you cannot appreciate a sunny day without the rain, you will not be able to appreciate your wins without your losses. Anything in life that is worthwhile will come with hardships so the sooner that you understand the importance of failing, the sooner you will be closer to reaching your goals. Resolve was emphasized in Chapter 2 for a reason. Without it, you are prone to giving up on your goal(s) the moment you encounter a hardship or if your plan does not go as intended. We are here to see you win and part of that means we must also prepare you for your loss. Keep striving to accomplish your goal(s) and don't be afraid if things don't work out as you initially intended. As long as you learn from the past you will get to the goal in due time. Learning to accept failure as a part of life will empower you beyond belief. The reason for this is that it enables you to learn from your failures.

CHAPTER 8

～⚬～

Tunnel Vision

On the journey to accomplishing goals, you will encounter many obstacles both internally as well as externally. The internal forces will differ from person to person, but some examples could include self-doubt, laziness, negative mindset, etc. External forces could include friends, family, work, etc. While it is impossible to prevent ALL obstacles, the one thing that you can control is how you respond to them. Like failure, obstacles and hardships are a part of life.

Realizing and embracing these facts of life will enable you to become steadfast in your resolve to keep pursuing your goal(s). Developing tunnel vision is one of the tools that will aid you on your journey. Tunnel vision means that you are hyper focused on your goal to the point where nothing can deter or distract you from it. This mindset is imperative to remaining on the path that you laid out.

Scenario: *You tend to get distracted with TV during the week and forget to do your homework.*

Example (not having tunnel vision): You set a goal to not watch any TV during the week and only watch 1 hour of TV a day on the weekends until the end of the semester. The first week went well and you became more productive in school. The second week, you still avoid watching TV during the week but then your favorite series releases a whole season. Over the weekend, you binge watch the entire season for hours. This behavior continues into the week, and you watch 30 minutes of TV twice a week but you do not think much of it. Your friends invite you over during the week to watch a new show and you skip out on your homework to go hang out. By the end of the semester, you realize you never really fixed your issue and you constantly procrastinate on getting assignments done. You struggle to keep up with the work and even have poor grades.

Example (having tunnel vision): You set a goal to not watch any TV during the week and only watch 1 hour of TV a day on the weekends until the end of the semester. The first week went well and you became more productive at school. Your favorite TV series releases an entire season. You remind yourself of how difficult it would be to turn the show off once you start watching; you make a decision to avoid the show all together until the end of the semester. Halfway through the semester you have developed a good focus on your goal and doing well with keeping up with your assignments. When your friends reach out to watch TV shows during the week, you politely decline. You end up keeping up with assignments and excelling in the semester.

This example demonstrates that you can achieve your goal by remaining focused and having tunnel vision. Think of this mindset as an important tool in your arsenal as distractions can derail you from your path. When you have tunnel vision, it can prevent you from experiencing avoidable disappointments and failures. Being successful on any avenue requires you to be aware of the tools that can aid you along the way. Tunnel vision does not mean that you should skip any steps listed in this book like embracing failures or pivoting when need be. The purpose of this chapter is to reaffirm that when you choose to set a goal, it is important to pursue it while blocking out the noise. Keep pushing forward until your goal(s) are obtained

but remember to measure your results along the way
and pivot as needed.

WISHING YOU WELL

The purpose of this chapter is to serve as a reminder to follow the steps that we have laid out as many times as needed until your goal is accomplished. It is natural that when we become comfortable with something that we begin to start looking for shortcuts to save on time. We're happy to let you know that as you get better with goal setting, you will be able to speed through this process as you master the fundamentals. With that said, we are cautiously informing you that it is not advised to skip any steps in this process as these are the critical steps to setting goals. Achieving greatness takes time and dedication so don't rush this process. Use this book as your guide to get things accomplished and remember that things will go wrong on your journey; brace yourself for the ride and continue pushing through the rough times. We believe in you, and we are here in spirit to cheer you towards greatness.

Workbook: Goal Setting

MY GOAL : _____

Overcoming the obstacles
. . . . . .

List potential obstacles
. . . . . .

Steps to measure results
. . . . . .

What is needed to start your plan?
. . . . .

How will you pivot after failure?
. . . . .

Why is this goal important?
. . . . . .

Start Date	End Date	My Plan			

MY GOAL : _____

Start Date	End Date	My Plan

Steps to measure results
· · · · · ·

List potential obstacles
· · · · · ·

Overcoming the obstacles
· · · · · ·

Why is this goal important?
· · · · · ·

What is needed to start your plan?
· · · · · ·

How will you pivot after failure?
· · · · · ·

Workbook: Goal Setting

MY GOAL : _____

Overcoming the obstacles
. . . . . .

List potential obstacles
. . . .

What is needed to start your plan?
. . . . . .

How will you pivot after failure?
. . . . . .

Steps to measure results

Why is this goal important?
. . . . . .

Start Date	End Date	My Plan

MY GOAL : Lose 8 lbs in 30 days

For illustration purposes only

Start Date	End Date	My Plan
07/01/21	07/31/21	Run 1 mile a day
07/01/21	07/31/21	Log 5,000 steps a day
07/01/21	07/31/21	Eat breakfast, lunch and dinner. NO SNACKS

Steps to measure results
- Check weight weekly
- Check fitness tracking device to ensure that I am taking 5,000 steps daily

List potential obstacles
- I love candy
- My family does not eat healthy
- Soda & juice

Overcoming the obstacles
- I will have plenty of water and sugar free gum to avoid candy
- I will help my family cook to encourage good habits
- I will not buy soda or juice
-

Why is this goal important?
- Want to be healthy overall
- Have my clothes fit me better
- Want to increase my self confidence

What is needed to start your plan?
- Mentally prepare myself for the road ahead
- Establish a baseline weight

How will you pivot after failure?
- If I fail, i will evaluate my eating and workout plan to demtermine how I can improve

37

Made in the USA
Middletown, DE
01 October 2021